# FUTURE SPACE

ROBOT EXPLORERS

Created and produced by Firecrest Books Ltd
in association with Alpha Communications and
Sebastian Quigley/Linden Artists


Copyright © 2003 Firecrest Books Ltd,
Alpha Communications, and
Sebastian Quigley/Linden Artists


Published by Tangerine Press, an imprint of Scholastic Inc.
557 Broadway, New York, NY 10012

ISBN 0-439-51809-1

Printed and bound in Thailand
First Printing 2003

# FUTURE SPACE

# ROBOT EXPLORERS

**David Jefferis**

Consultant **Mat Irvine, FBIS**

Illustrated by **Sebastian Quigley**

Tangerine Press and associated logo and
design are trademarks of Scholastic Inc.

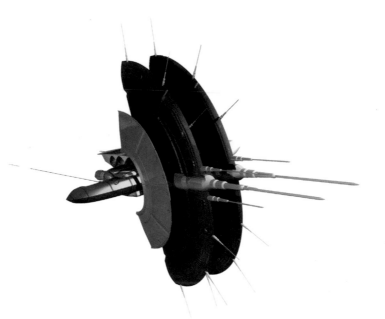

Consultant
**Mat Irvine, FBIS**

Publishing Consultant
**Peter Sackett**

Designer and Art Director
**Phil Jacobs**

Editor
**Norman Barrett**

Project Coordinator
**Pat Jacobs**

Color separation in Singapore by
**SC International Pte Ltd.**

Printed in Thailand by
**Sirivatana Interprint Public Co. Ltd.**

# CONTENTS

# ROBOTS IN SPACE

The Space Age dawned on October 4, 1957, when the first successful spacecraft – a Russian satellite called Sputnik 1 – was fired into Earth's orbit, a curving path in space around our planet. Sputnik 1 was a shiny metal globe weighing 184 pounds (83.5 kg). It proved to be the first of many thousands of spacecraft to be launched into space.

## Exploring the universe

Since the days of Sputnik 1, robot craft (ones that are unmanned, and depend on computers to control their missions) have explored space around the Moon, the Sun, the Earth, and all of the other planets, except the most distant one – tiny, frozen Pluto. Robot probes have also explored other space objects, such as asteroid "space rocks" and "dirty snowball" comets. More than a dozen countries have launched spacecraft, including the United States, Russia, China, India, and Japan. Many other countries work together on international teams, such as the European Space Agency (ESA).

## Two types of robot explorer

Unmanned spacecraft come in two main types. Earth satellites follow an orbit around our planet. Cameras and other sensors enable them to do such jobs as checking the weather or pollution. Spaceprobes are sent beyond Earth to the Moon, planets, and even deep space. Their job is to find out about the vast universe we live in and the great beyond.

*The Solar System is the name for the planets, moons, and other cosmic material that circle in space around the Sun. All the planets, except Mercury and Venus, have moons circling them. The numbers vary, from Earth's single Moon to more than 50 orbiting Jupiter.*

*Spaceprobes have been sent on robot explorer missions for roughly half a century. In that time, scientists have learned much about our space neighborhood.*

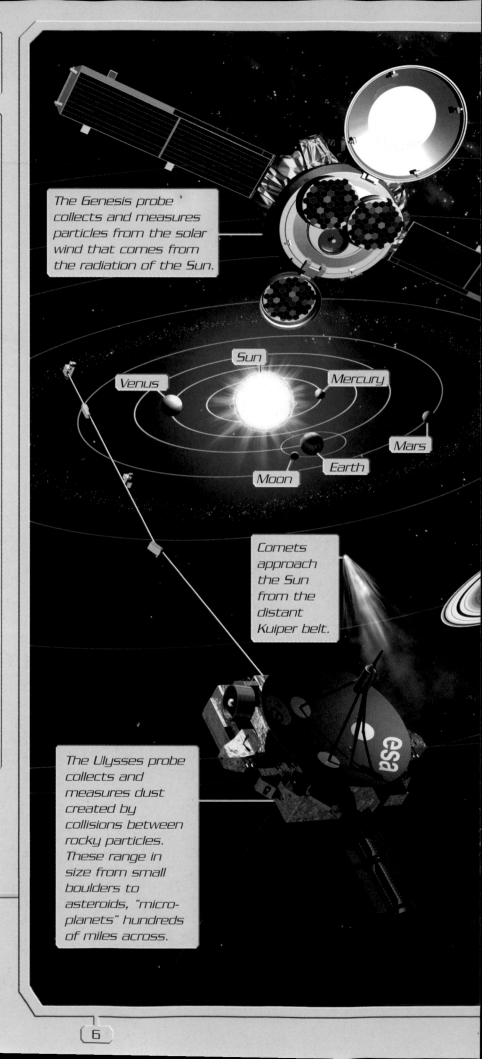

The Genesis probe collects and measures particles from the solar wind that comes from the radiation of the Sun.

Sun

Venus

Mercury

Mars

Earth

Moon

Comets approach the Sun from the distant Kuiper belt.

The Ulysses probe collects and measures dust created by collisions between rocky particles. These range in size from small boulders to asteroids, "micro-planets" hundreds of miles across.

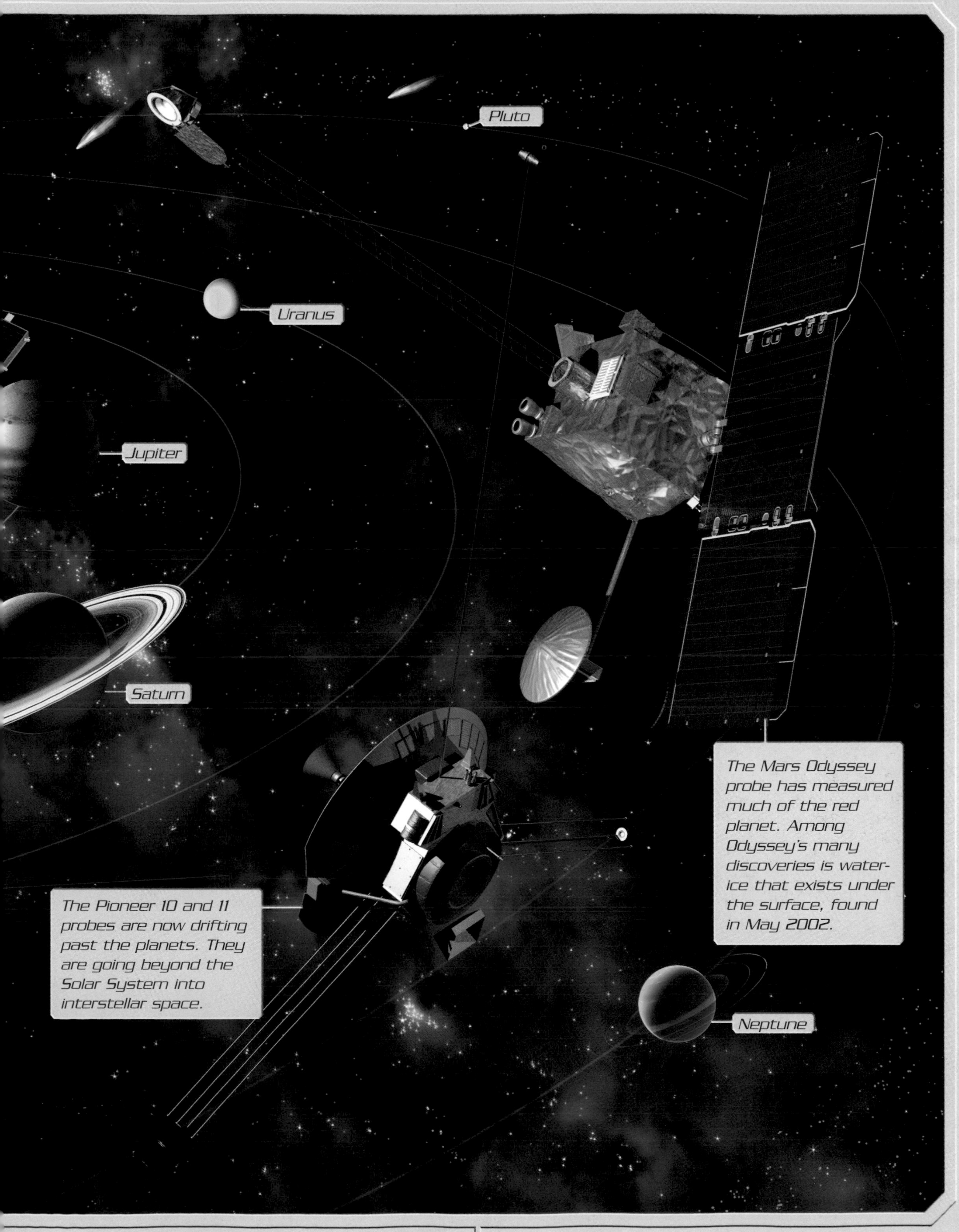

Pluto

Uranus

Jupiter

Saturn

Neptune

The Mars Odyssey probe has measured much of the red planet. Among Odyssey's many discoveries is water-ice that exists under the surface, found in May 2002.

The Pioneer 10 and 11 probes are now drifting past the planets. They are going beyond the Solar System into interstellar space.

# EXPLORING PLANET EARTH

Satellites orbiting the Earth help us check on our world. They show details that are impossible to see at ground level. "Earth-sensing" robots date back to 1960, when the U.S. Tiros weather satellite was launched into space. Cameras aboard Tiros showed mostly clouds, but the black-and-white pictures also revealed unexpected patterns in the snowy regions of Canada. Experts studied the patterns closely and realized that they showed where lumberjacks had cleared forests. Since then, cameras have been developed to pick up very fine detail – the most advanced equipment can see headlines on a newspaper!

## Checking the environment

One of the biggest Earth-sensing satellites is Envisat, built by a European science team and launched by the huge Ariane 5 rocket from a base at Kourou in South America. Envisat measures nearly 23 feet (7 m) long, similar in size to a delivery truck. The spacecraft carries equipment that is designed to record many important aspects of our planet.

Envisat's radar beams can punch through clouds to record what's happening at ground level. They could be used to probe drifting icebergs, the health of a forest, or the spread of a desert. Other equipment on Envisat can measure vehicle pollution, dust storms, factory waste, and ash clouds from erupting volcanoes. The satellite may help to plan and control disaster relief efforts by checking on the progress of floods, fires, and earthquakes.

*Envisat orbits just over 500 miles (800 km) above the Earth.*

*Radar antenna*

*Envisat was assembled for flight in the Netherlands (inset right). Further right is the ground antenna in Italy that communicates with Envisat.*

*Pictures at top right:*
*A  Smoke rises from the volcano Mt. Etna, on the island of Sicily.*
*B  Rivers and clouds show up clearly as Envisat takes pictures above the coast of West Africa.*
*C  Ice floes drift in the sea as they break off the edge of Antarctica.*

Radio antenna

Envisat takes 100 minutes to complete an orbit. In three days it can map the entire Earth.

© ESA 2002

A

B

© ESA 2002

C

Fold-out solar panel

# MOON PROBES

The first craft to land on the Moon was the Russian Luna 2. In September 1959, this 860 pound (390 kg) probe crashed into the lunar surface. It was not a carefully controlled "soft" landing, but reaching the Moon at all was a big success in the 1950s. Early rockets were unreliable, and so were their guidance systems. The Moon is 239,000 miles (384,000 km) away and moves constantly in its orbit around the Earth, so homing in on such a target was a triumph for Russia.

## Moon rover

Other spaceprobes and soft-landers followed the lead of Luna 2, but the first robot Moon rover didn't arrive until November 1970, more than a year after the first U.S. astronauts had walked on the surface, in July 1969. Russia's Lunokhod 1 rover looked more like an old-fashioned coffee-machine than a piece of high-tech equipment. But the eight-wheeled robot was very reliable, and rolled slowly around for more than 10 months, sending back many pictures of the surface.

## Future plans

There has been little Moon exploration since the Apollo missions in the 1970s, but many scientists think it's time to go back. Among the probes planned, the Japanese Lunar-A, a craft that will fire spear-like penetrators toward the Moon to punch through the surface and create a number of mini-Moonquakes. By measuring the vibrations of these, scientists should be able to find out what the moon is made of.

**The European Smart-1 probe should travel near the Moon for about six months. It has a new type of engine that can fire for weeks at a time, gradually building up speed.**

**Japan's Lunar-A carries a group of penetrator probes close to the Moon. They are designed to smash into the lunar surface at very high speed.**

**The 87-inch (221-cm) Lunokhod 1 of 1970 carried TV cameras and other items of research equipment. Its batteries were recharged by solar cells on the folding lid.**

*Lunar-A releases penetrator probe 25 miles (40 km) above the Moon.*

*Lunar-A has a camera that can photograph objects on the Moon as small as 100 feet (30 m) across.*

*Rocket motor slows down penetrator from moon orbit, to fall toward the surface.*

Penetrator falls free when its rocket burns out at 15 miles (25 km) above the surface.

As planned, two penetrators will be aimed at sites on the Moon's nearside, two more at sites on the far side.

Instruments on the penetrator send details to Lunar-A, which sends the information back to scientists on Earth.

Penetrator hits the surface at 683 mph (1,100 km/h).

Depending on how hard the soil is at the impact point, the penetrator will dig in about 3 to 10 feet (1-3 m).

# SUN STORM

The Sun is our nearest star, and all life on Earth depends on its regular supply of heat and light. And yet, for all its importance, scientists do not know exactly how the Sun works, nor can they predict solar flares accurately. These are great eruptions on the Sun's surface. One such explosion in 1973 blew a vast cloud of helium gas 350,000 miles (563,000 km) into space in just 90 seconds. Other flares send plumes of deadly radiation into space, enough to kill an unprotected astronaut, or destroy delicate computer circuits. On Earth, changes in the Sun's energy may affect the weather and how well food crops grow. For these reasons, as well as scientific interest, various robot explorers have been sent to study the Sun since the 1960s. One of the latest solar probes is called Soho.

## Solar observatory
The Soho probe is a U.S./European team effort. It was sent into space from Cape Canaveral, Florida, in December 1995 and has been studying the Sun ever since. Using its daily observations, researchers have been able to plot solar storms and eruptions, and improve their chances of forecasting such events before they happen. But things have not always gone smoothly. In 1998, the probe went mysteriously silent with more than four months passing before engineers managed to fix the problem.

## Over the poles
Another solar probe is called Ulysses. It has been in space since 1990 and cruises in five year looping orbits, high above and below the Sun. From its orbit, it can observe and measure events in areas around the Sun's north and south poles.

**The Sun is a vast ball of burning gas that is nearly 865,000 miles (1.39 million km) across. It dwarfs even Jupiter and Saturn, the biggest planets.**

**An immense cloud of gases form a massive solar prominence in the Sun's upper chromosphere. This one lasted for about four hours.**

*Solar flares and prominences loop into space far and fast. Soho has measured gases speeding along at more than 2 million mph (3 million km/h).*

*Soho orbits in space 1 million miles (1.6 million km) nearer the Sun than the Earth. From here, it has an uninterrupted view.*

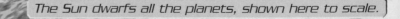
The Sun dwarfs all the planets, shown here to scale.

Solar-cell "wings" generate power to run Soho's cameras and other instruments.

Temperature at the Sun's surface is about 11,000° F (6000° C).

Soho carries 12 instruments that measure the Sun's surface, its flares and storms. Soho can also detect comets in space. By February 2000, the probe had spotted more than 100 comets.

Soho's structure is 14 feet (4.3 m) long. The solar cells span just over 31 feet (9.5 m). The craft weighs 4,080 pounds (1,850 kg).

Earth

**8:03**     **9:53**     **11:15**     **11:31**

**11:35**     **11:42**     **11:55**     **12:10**

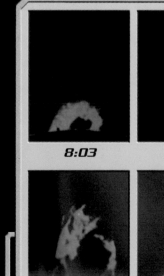

# JOURNEYS IN SPACE AND TIME

The Hubble Space Telescope (HST) is a school bus-sized observatory that views the heavens as it orbits around the Earth, above the blurring effects of dust and pollution in our atmosphere.

HST was sent into space in 1990 and has operated continuously ever since, except when being serviced by astronauts from a Space Shuttle.

## Time viewer

Traveling at 186,000 miles a second (300,000 km/sec), light takes just over eight minutes to reach Earth, so at any one moment sunlight is eight minutes "old" by the time it gets here. Light from the farthest stars that HST can view takes many millions of years to reach us, making HST's pictures of them snapshots of the past as well as of space. HST's farthest images show objects as they were when the universe was much younger, allowing researchers to learn how the universe has aged over the years.

## Spectacular views

HST has taken thousands of pictures since launch, including views of other planets in our Solar System, distant stars, and clouds of glowing gas so huge that the Earth would look dwarfed by comparison. There are plans for an improved HST, called the James Webb Space Telescope (JWST). This will see even farther into space. Researchers have already found dozens of "exo-planets" – worlds orbiting other stars, but so far these have all been much bigger than the Earth. One of the jobs for the JWST will be to look for smaller, Earth-sized exo-planets.

*The James Webb Space Telescope will have protective shields that fold out like a pair of giant fans.*

*Astronauts on a servicing mission work on upgrading HST's systems.*

*Images from HST: (A) A galaxy with stars being born from dust and gas; (B) Remains of an exploding star; (C) The planet Mars in spring and autumn; (D) Views of the planet Saturn, taken from 1996 to 2000.*

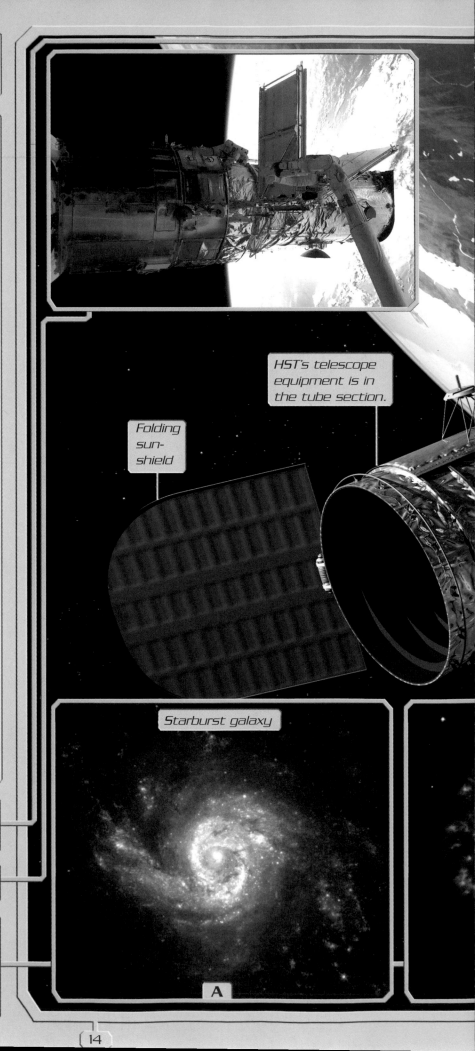

HST's telescope equipment is in the tube section.

Folding sun-shield

Starburst galaxy

A

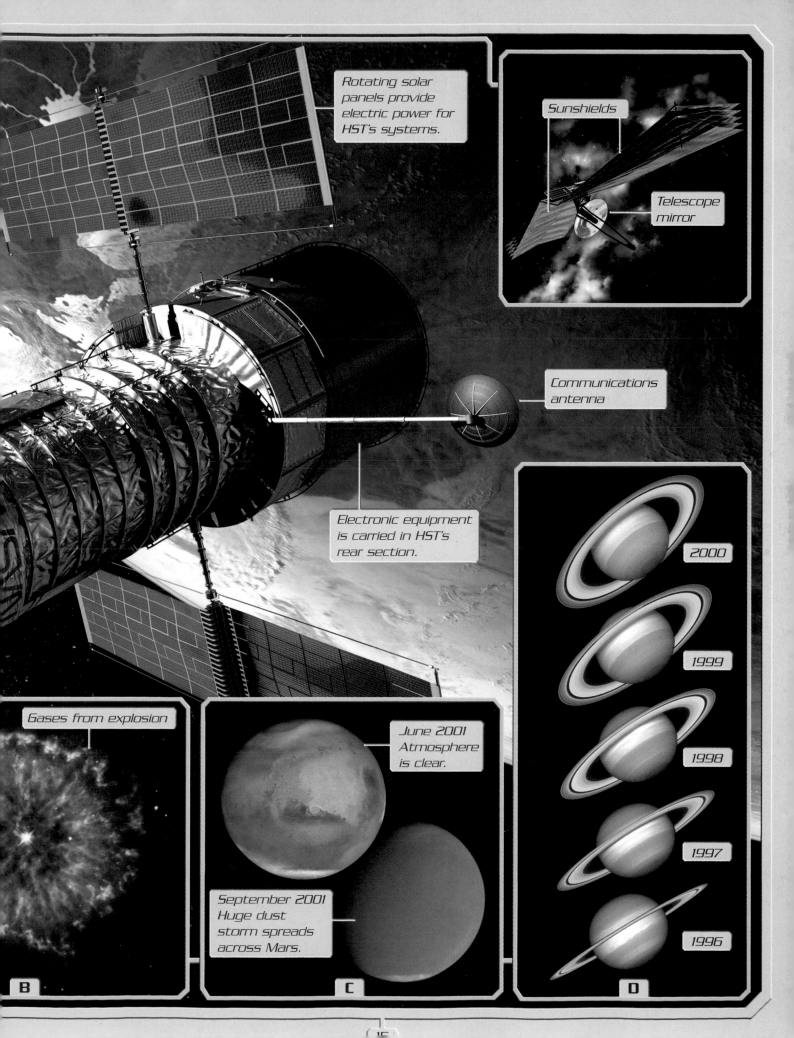

Rotating solar panels provide electric power for HST's systems.

Sunshields

Telescope mirror

Communications antenna

Electronic equipment is carried in HST's rear section.

Gases from explosion

June 2001 Atmosphere is clear.

September 2001 Huge dust storm spreads across Mars.

2000

1999

1998

1997

1996

B

C

D

# CRATER PLANET

Mercury is the planet nearest the Sun, moving in an orbit just 36 million miles (58 million km) from our local star. With days and nights that each last nearly two Earth-months, Mercury gets very hot and very cold. At high noon, you would be fried at a sizzling 620°F (327°C). Standing in the same spot at midnight, you would freeze at a chilly 298°F (-183°C).

## Mariner flies by

So far, just one spaceprobe has been close to Mercury. In 1974, cameras aboard the U.S. Mariner 10 probe showed an airless, Moon-like world packed full of craters, mountains, and plains. The biggest crater was named the Caloris Basin, and is 807 miles (1,300 km) across. Researchers think it was made millions of years ago, when a giant meteor crashed into the planet.

## Future explorer

Mariner 10 was a great success, but it mapped only one-third of Mercury's rugged terrain. So a new probe, called Messenger, is being prepared for a close-up mission, due for launch in 2004. Messenger will help us learn more about this mysterious, dead world. In 2008, the probe will make two fly-bys, then go into orbit around Mercury for a year or more. During this time, Messenger will complete the maps started by Mariner 10, check what the planet is made of and other measurements.

**The Messenger probe will swoop close to Mercury in two passes. Special sunshields will keep the probe cool enough to work correctly this close to the Sun.**

**Mercury is a small planet, about halfway between the Earth and Moon in size. It is just 3,030 miles (4,878 km) across.**

**Mariner 10 sent back more than 2,500 pictures of Mercury. The smallest craters were less than 300 feet (100 m) across.**

Solar panels provide electricity to run systems aboard Messenger.

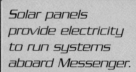

Earth

Moon

Mercury

A thermal shade protects Messenger's delicate instruments from the intense heat of the Sun.

Messenger will orbit Mercury at a height of just 120 miles (200 km) at its lowest point.

As planned, Messenger will stay in orbit around Mercury for about a year.

Cameras will be able to take pictures of the parts of Mercury that have not been seen before.

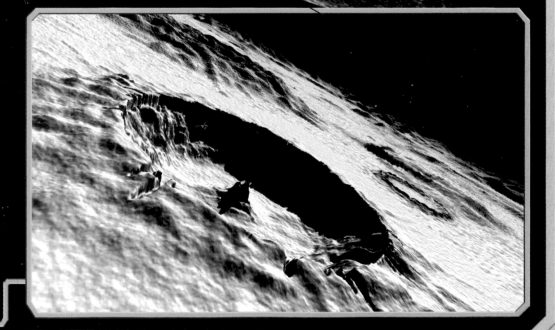

# FURNACE WORLD

The Romans named Venus after their goddess of love because it was the brightest of the planets known to the Romans. Until the first spaceprobes traveled to Venus, many experts thought it might be like a warmer, lusher version of Earth. Venus is nearer the Sun, so they thought it might have a tropical climate and warm oceans, perhaps with steamy jungles and heat-loving reptiles living under the thick clouds that hide the surface.

## Deadly findings

Two Russian Venera spaceprobes made the first successful landings on Venus, in the 1970s. They confirmed readings made by earlier, fly-by probes. At the surface, the heat was twice that of a kitchen oven running at top temperature. The choking atmosphere was filled with deadly sulfuric acid, and the pressure was many times that on Earth. An astronaut landing on Venus would be boiled, squashed, and dunked in acid, all at the same time!

## Russian and U.S. probes

So far, the only robots to land on the hot surface of Venus have been the Russian Venera probes. They sent back a few images of the surface. In 1989, the U.S. Magellan probe went on a five-year mission. It did not land, instead staying in orbit around Venus, using radar beams to penetrate the clouds. Magellan mapped all but small areas of the furnace planet.

**Earth (left) and Venus are almost the same size, but the similarity ends there. Venus has no oceans, and the surface roasts at an average temperature of 896°F (480°C).**

**The U.S. Magellan spaceprobe was launched from the cargo bay of a U.S. Space Shuttle. Using advanced radar equipment, the probe mapped most of Venus from orbit.**

**Russia's Venera landers could send pictures to Earth for only a short time after landing on Venus, in 1978.**

Earth

Venus

*The Venera lander was carried to Venus' orbit by a larger craft, then released on a one-way trip to the surface.*

Pipes carried cooling fluid from the orbiter to the lander.

Antenna for sending signals to the orbiter, which sent the information to Earth.

This metal disk helped slow the capsule down through the thick atmosphere.

Camera system for taking pictures

Insulated metal sphere kept the equipment inside cool for a time.

Shock absorber took the force of a heavy landing on the hot surface.

# EXPLORING THE RED PLANET

The planet Mars is a world of rust-red deserts, dust storms, and icy polar regions. In summer, days can be as warm as 60°F (16°C), but nights are way below freezing. The air is thinner than at the top of Earth's highest mountain, so any future astronauts will need suits with breathing gear and heaters. Even so, Mars is the most Earth-like of the other planets in the Solar System.

## Target: red planet

In 1997, the U.S. sent a wheeled rover to Mars. It was nicknamed "Rocky" and was about the size of a microwave oven. The little machine was a great success, and other probes will be launched in the future. The U.S./Europe Beagle 2 is a small lander-probe designed to look for life-signs. Its equipment includes a mini-drill to dig into the soil. Beagle 2 stands a good chance of finding any life on Mars.

## Hunting for aliens

Researchers don't expect to meet any "bug-eyed monsters" on Mars, but there may be remains of ancient bacteria or even fossilized sea creatures. The U.S. Mars Global Surveyor probe found water under the surface, mixed with the soil. It is likely that millions of years ago, Mars did have seas and oceans. Researchers think that there is currently enough water-ice on the planet to make an ankle-deep ocean if it all melted.

In 1976, two U.S. Viking probes circled Mars, while sending landers down to the sandy surface. Each lander carried a mini-laboratory to test for signs of life, but they found no convincing evidence.

The U.S. 2003 Mars rovers were built with metal wheels, a set of cameras, and equipment to carry out various tests on the Martian environment.

Ideas for future Mars explorations include equipment carried aboard balloons, planes, and various landers.

Mars has a pinkish sky, caused by sandy dust in the thin atmosphere.

Antenna

Rover's top speed on level ground is about 2 inches (5 cm) per second.

Antenna

Equipment that needs to be kept warm is contained in the probe's body section.

Each 10-inch (25-cm) wheel has its own electric motor.

Cameras can turn and tilt for wide views across the dusty Marscape.

Solar panels generate electricity during the Martian day.

Front cameras

Metal wheels have spiky treads for gripping the rough ground.

The robot arm's equipment includes the RAT (Rock Abrasion Tool). This grinds a hole 0.2 inch (5 mm) deep, so a rock's interior can be examined.

Viking orbiter

Viking lander was carried in a protective aeroshell.

Arm digs into soil.

Beagle 2 was built in Europe and flown on a U.S. rocket. It was designed to drill into the Mars soil to test it for signs of life.

Balloon probe

Aircraft probe

Lightweight lander probe

# ASTEROID EXPLORER

Asteroids are chunks of rock, moving through space. They are thought to be "rubble," left over from the formation of the planets billions of years ago. Asteroids range from tiny "space pebbles" less than a mile across to the biggest known, called Ceres. But even Ceres is not very large. It is about 600 miles (1,000 km) across, less than one-third the size of our Moon. Astronauts have not been to an asteroid, but the spaceprobe NEAR-Shoemaker visited a small one called Eros in 2000.

## Rock in space

Eros is an oval rock just 21 miles (34 km) long. It has very feeble gravity – a child weighing 75 pounds (34 kg) on Earth would weigh only about 0.75 ounce (21 g) on Eros. One big jump and you could fly off into space! Such a small asteroid made a tiny target for NEAR-Shoemaker, but after a 196 million mile (316 million km) journey, the probe successfully went into close orbit. After NEAR-Shoemaker had taken lots of pictures, scientists directed the probe to a gentle crash-landing on the surface. It even sent out a signal after the crash!

## Bringing back a sample

The Japanese hope to bring back a piece of asteroid in a few years time. As planned, the Muses-C probe will arrive at a nameless asteroid, identified only by its number (25413) 1998SF36. The probe will aim to land, dig a sample, then bring it back to Earth. Such a sample may supply clues to the early history of the Solar System.

*The NEAR-Shoemaker probe is the only probe so far to have made a close encounter with an asteroid.*

*Asteroids sometimes hit planets – and many researchers think that a big one could have brought the dinosaurs to extinction millions of years ago. A direct hit would boil oceans, make huge tidal waves, and affect the weather for decades.*

*We may need to protect Earth in the future. Here spacecraft leave on a mission to divert an asteroid on a collision course with our planet.*

Solar panels generate electricity.

Gold foil insulates the probe's main body from the extremes of heat and cold in space.

Thruster jets keep probe at the correct angle.

Eros looks like a large rocky potato. It is about 21 miles (34 km) long and 8 miles (13 km) across.

There is no danger of Eros ever hitting Earth, but some asteroids do come close. In June 2002, an asteroid passed within 75,000 miles 120,000 km. less than one-third of the distance to the Moon.

Antenna for communicating with controllers back on Earth

Eros turns slowly in space. A day there lasts just under five and a half hours.

The surface of Eros is pitted with thousands of craters.

# COMET CHASER

Asteroids are not the only pieces of cosmic rubble in the sky. There are also countless numbers of comets, drifting in the dark. Comets are thought to be "dirty snowballs," with a rocky core, or nucleus, mixed with ice, dust, and frozen gases. Comets drift in the chilly outer Solar System, but occasionally one loops nearer the Sun. When this happens, the Sun's heat may boil off some of the material, and then a huge, shining tail may form. The tail is made of ultra-fine material. One estimate says that a million-mile (1.6 million km) tail has only enough solid matter in it to fill a medium-sized suitcase!

## Comet collision

The first robot to explore a comet zone was the Giotto probe of 1986, which flew near the famous Halley's comet. Today the U.S. Stardust spaceprobe is chasing another comet, called Wild 2. Stardust was launched in February 1999 and has been gradually catching up with Wild 2. By April 2002, the spaceprobe had traveled more than 1.25 billion miles (2 billion km). By early 2004, Stardust should be on target, ready to fly straight through the comet's tail, catching some dust as it goes, and then returning to Earth with the sample.

## Rosetta lander

Rosetta is a future mission that plans to land on a comet and bring back a chunk of the nucleus.

*Stardust flies through the tail of comet Wild 2. The comet's material is left over from the birth of the Solar System, so a sample may show scientists what conditions were like millions of years ago.*

*Stardust mission diary:*
*(A) Stardust launch February 7, 1999.*
*(B) Featherlight material, called aerogel, is used to catch a comet sample on January 2, 2004.*
*(C) Sample returns in a capsule in January 2006.*
*(D) Capsule found by search team.*

*The Rosetta lander touches down on a chilly comet nucleus and gathers a sample for return to Earth.*

*Aerogel is mounted on flip-up arm.*

*When collected, the comet sample is placed inside this capsule for return to Earth.*

*Solar panels provide electricity for instruments.*

A

B

Here the comet nucleus is still far away. Cameras on Stardust guide the probe as close as possible.

Shields provide protection from comet dust passing at 13,650 mph (22,000 km/h).

Antenna for communicating with Earth

Rosetta lander

C

D

# EXPLORING GAS GIANTS

Beyond Mars are four huge worlds, giant balls of gas far larger than Earth. Biggest of them all is Jupiter, a vast planet criss-crossed with bands of clouds. Jupiter's Great Red Spot is a swirling storm big enough to swallow the Earth several times over. It has been raging for over 300 years. Jupiter also has more moons than other planets. By 2003, researchers found at least 52, and there could still be more.

## Target Jupiter

Robot explorers have been to Jupiter several times. In the 1970s, Pioneer and Voyager probes took close-up pictures of the planet and its moons. The U.S. Galileo probe spent the most time in the region. In 1995, the craft released a probe into Jupiter's thick atmosphere. It parachuted safely through the upper layers of gas, but the probe was crushed as it fell into the hidden depths below. As far as we know, Jupiter has no Earth-like solid surface, and what happened to the probe is unknown. After that, Galileo mapped many of the moons, and ended its mission by following its probe, blazing a trail into Jupiter's atmosphere in 2003.

## Future flyer

There are no firm plans for a follow-up to Galileo, but one idea is a Ju-plane. This will be a small aircraft that could cruise through Jupiter's clouds, sucking in hydrogen gas and using it for fuel.

*The "gas-giants" of the Solar System are Jupiter, Saturn, Uranus, and Neptune. They are all a lot larger than our planet – 1,300 Earths could fit inside Jupiter, with room to spare.*

*This concept shows a future robot craft designed to fly in Jupiter's atmosphere. Hydrogen gas is sucked into the nose intake, then burned as fuel. It would need no refueling and could fly for many years.*

*Dateline 1995: the Galileo spacecraft releases its probe on a one-way mission to drop into the swirling clouds of Jupiter.*

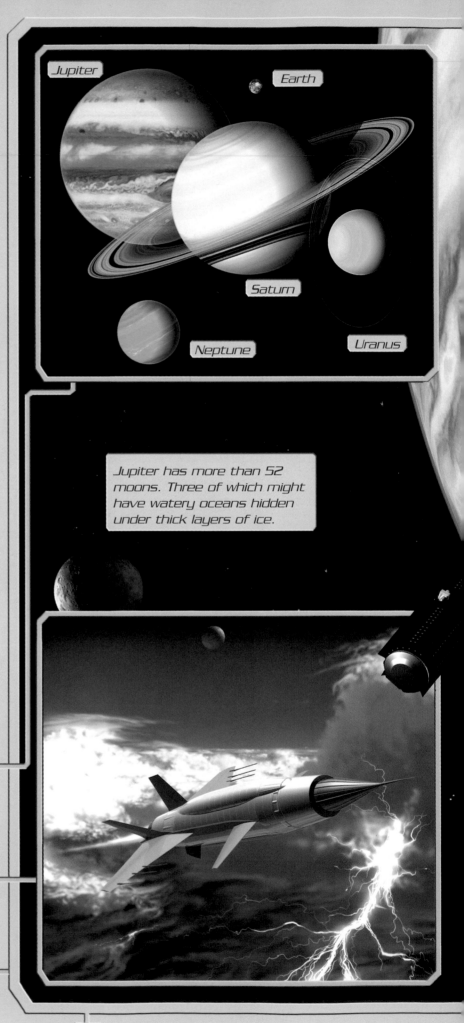

Jupiter    Earth

Saturn

Neptune    Uranus

*Jupiter has more than 52 moons. Three of which might have watery oceans hidden under thick layers of ice.*

Antenna communicates with Earth.

After a 14-year mission, Galileo was directed into the atmosphere of Jupiter in September 2003. This avoided a possible future collision with one of the moons.

Generators on two booms provide electric power.

Antenna communicates with atmosphere probe.

Probe fell through the outer layers of Jupiter's atmosphere, taking measurements for nearly an hour before being crushed.

Sensors measure Jupiter's magnetic field.

Great Red Spot

# SPACE SUBMARINE

In 2002, researchers tested an experimental probe called a "cryobot" on Spitzbergen Island, in the Arctic Ocean. The cryobot was designed to go through solid ice. But instead of using a powerful motor to turn a drill bit, the probe had a heating system that allowed it to melt through the ice. During the test, cryobot slid smoothly to a depth of 75 feet (23 m) under the surface. Its success may pave the way for a future version that could explore under the frozen surface of Europa, one of Jupiter's moons.

## Signs of life?

Scientists have been interested in Europa since seeing pictures taken by the Galileo spaceprobe. These show that Europa might have a watery ocean, trapped under a thick, icy cover. And some scientists think that, where there is water, there may be life.

## Going down

If built, a Europa probe would consist of three main sections, or modules. The first of these would stay in orbit, flying above Europa, where it would release a second module, the cryobot lander. This would melt its way through the ice – 12 miles (19 km) thick in parts – while trailing a radio and TV cable from the surface. Once under the ice, the cryobot would release its cargo, the third module. This is a micro-sized robot submarine, built to leave the cryobot to search the surrounding waters for signs of strange creatures living in this hidden world.

*The ice-covered, mini-world of Europa is 1,941 miles (3,124 km) across, a little smaller than Earth's Moon.*

*The cryobot stops once it has melted through the ice. A communications cable leads to the surface, where a low-power antenna sends information to the orbiter. This uses a stronger transmitter to relay details back to Earth. On Earth, underwater hot-spots are made by ocean-bottom volcanoes. Whole communities of animals, such as strange worms and blind crabs, live near them.*

*Lines show where ice has cracked and refrozen many times.*

*Europa is Jupiter's second-largest moon.*

*If found, Europa's life could be much like the worms and other simple creatures living on the ocean floors of planet Earth.*

Underside of Europa's icy covering

Cryobot stops when it has melted through the ice.

Propeller system moves robo-sub forward and backward.

Steering fins allow the robo-sub to maneuver underwater.

Cameras and other sensors are mounted in the nose section.

Boiling gases and red-hot lava flowing from ocean-floor volcanoes make the water around them warm.

# LANDING ON TITAN

Saturn, its beautiful rings, and many moons have already been explored by several probes. The U.S./Europe Cassini-Huygens mission is heading there now. The main spacecraft is named Cassini after the Italian astronomer who spotted gaps between Saturn's rings, in 1675. It carries a smaller probe, also named after an early astronomer, Christiaan Huygens.

## Mystery target

The Huygens probe is designed to see under the veil of the mystery world Titan, Saturn's largest moon. This large moon is bigger than Mercury and Pluto, and has a thick atmosphere of misty, chemical smog that earlier probes were unable to see through. Some researchers think that the surface conditions may be similar to those on Earth billions of years ago, but much colder. Daytime temperatures on Titan are -298°F (-183°C), because Titan is much farther from the Sun than we are, so it receives little heat. If Huygens finds any life it will be unlike anything we can imagine.

## Flight plan

The Cassini-Huygens mission took off from Cape Canaveral, Florida, in October 1997. After cruising through space for nearly seven years, the spaceprobe should reach Saturn in July 2004. A few months later, the Huygens lander will be released, to parachute down through the thick clouds of Titan to a soft landing on a new world.

*Technicians prepare Cassini-Huygens for launch. They work in "clean-room" conditions to make sure the probe is in perfect condition for flight.*

*The Cassini orbiter releases the Huygens lander probe. Huygens will hurtle through Titan's outer atmosphere before being slowed by parachutes for a soft landing.*

*Huygens starts its research on Titan. This picture shows Saturn rising, but in reality Titan's thick clouds may hide the view.*

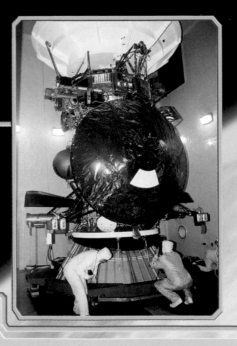

*Saturn is far bigger than the Earth. It has a diameter of nearly 75,000 miles (120,000 km).*

*The Cassini spaceprobe relays signals from the lander to Earth, using a very powerful radio system.*

Saturn's rings are made of countless chunks of ice, ranging in size from dust grains to house-sized boulders.

Saturn has at least 30 moons. Cassini may find more smaller ones.

Titan is the largest moon in the Solar System, with a diameter of 3,200 miles (5,150 km).

The Huygens lander is carried inside this cone-shaped aeroshell until it has slowed down in Titan's atmosphere. Then the lander separates for touchdown.

# GRAND TOUR

Some robot explorers visit more than a single target. Back in the 1970s, mission planners realized they could give a spaceprobe aimed at Jupiter a "free" ride to worlds beyond, using the giant planet's gravity to boost the probe past in a high-speed fly-by. And the gravity of the next planet could propel it even farther. This plan meant that a robot explorer could cruise on a Grand Tour of two or more outer worlds during a single mission.

## Voyagers are launched

In 1977, two Voyager spaceprobes were fired into space, a few weeks apart. Voyager 1 flew past Jupiter and Saturn, but Voyager 2 carried out a four planet Grand Tour. In 1979, it flew by Jupiter, and two years later Saturn. A boost from the ringed planet allowed the probe to fly by Uranus in 1986. Three years after that, Voyager 2 skimmed just 3,000 miles (4,800 km) above misty-blue Neptune. During its 12-year mission, Voyager 2 sent back thousands of images and made detailed readings of conditions in the outer Solar System.

## Beyond the planets

Today the Voyagers are far beyond the planets of this solar system to the unknown region between the stars. By the year 2020, Voyager 1 will be more than 12 billion miles (19 billion km) from the Sun, with Voyager 2 following behind. Soon after that, fuel and power supplies carried on the probes will run out. Then the silent machines will drift into the depths of the universe.

*Voyager 2 passes close to Neptune's moon, Triton. The probe spotted huge geysers of chilly nitrogen gas erupting from the surface. Sunlight is very weak in these distant regions. Daylight on Triton is about 900 times dimmer than on Earth.*

*Four spaceprobes have gone beyond the planets. Pioneers 10 and 11 flew Jupiter missions earlier than the Voyagers. All four are heading out in different directions. The Pioneers are now silent, but the Voyagers still transmit information to Earth.*

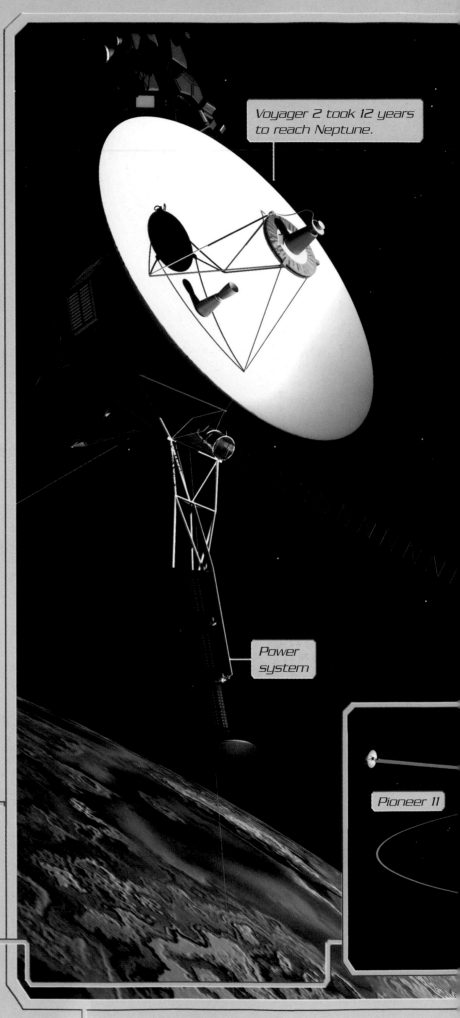

*Voyager 2 took 12 years to reach Neptune.*

Power system

Pioneer 11

The Great Dark Spot
(GDS) is a huge storm in
Neptune's atmosphere.

Neptune has rings, but
they are very faint,
unlike those of Saturn.

Neptune has a diameter of
30,750 miles (49,500 km),
about four times wider
than the Earth.

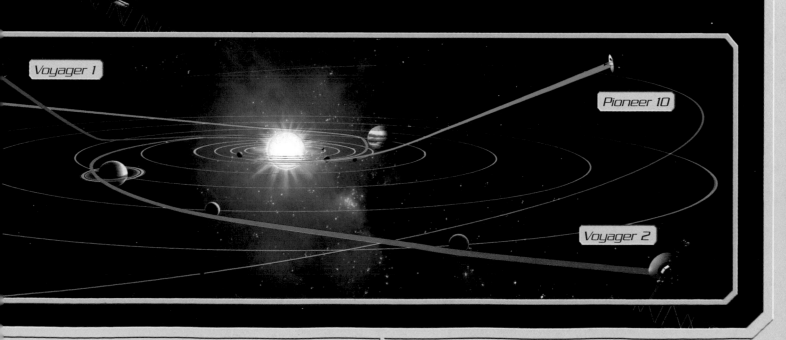

Voyager 1

Pioneer 10

Voyager 2

# NEW HORIZONS

There is only one planet in the Solar System left unexplored – distant Pluto and its moon, Charon. Pluto is the farthest planet from the Sun, but was in the wrong position for a visit by the Voyagers.

Now there are plans for a mission to Pluto, called the New Horizons probe. As planned, a 20-year-plus flight will start from Earth in 2006. A fly-by past Jupiter will boost the probe to a top speed of 50,000 mph (80,000 km/h), after which its next target is Pluto. The probe should arrive there in 2015.

## Close encounter

Not much is known about Pluto and Charon, though blurry pictures taken by the Hubble Space Telescope have shown parts of Pluto that are darker than coal, while others are brighter than snow. It's likely that there are ice-fields of frozen gases, with the temperature hundreds of degrees below zero. Voyager 2 found ice-geysers on Triton, and New Horizons may find similar things on Charon, but perhaps even stranger things are there, waiting to be discovered!

## Going farther

Beyond Pluto, the New Horizons probe will keep heading out, its new target to inspect a Kuiper Belt Object (KBO), one of millions of small icy objects thought to exist beyond the planets. It's the area where many comets come from, so checking out a KBO is a fascinating target for researchers. But it's a long journey, and the probe is not expected to pass near a KBO until about 2026.

*The New Horizons spaceprobe flies past Pluto. Charon appears as a crescent against the distant Sun as the probe speeds by.*

*Pluto is very small – it's not even as big as Earth's Moon. Some scientists believe Pluto is too tiny to be called a planet.*

*Pluto's icy surface may look like this. There are some misty clouds in the sky, but the atmosphere is 100,000 times less dense than on Earth. It is so cold that you would freeze in a few seconds.*

*Charon is Pluto's only moon. It rotates much more slowly than Earth – a day on Charon lasts more than 140 hours.*

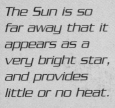

*The Sun is so far away that it appears as a very bright star, and provides little or no heat.*

Earth

Moon

Pluto

Charon

Cameras are able to photograph objects on Pluto about as small as 200 feet (60 m) across.

Electricity generating module

Powerful antenna sends signals back to Earth.

New Horizons will speed past Pluto during a 24-hour fly-by. The closest approach will be about 6,000 miles (9,600 km) above the surface.

# STAR SAILOR

When our Solar System has been explored, the next destination for robots will be the nearest star system, Alpha Centauri. It's a long way – light from our local star, the Sun, takes over 8 minutes to reach the Earth, but the light from Alpha Centauri takes over 4 years to get here! For a normal spaceprobe, it is an impossible journey that would take thousands of years.

## Microwave flyer

Scientist Robert L. Forward has come up with a scheme for a probe that might be possible to build one day. He calls the design Starwisp. It consists of a sheet of ultra-fine wires in the form of a sail over half a mile (1 km) wide. The probe's construction would be feather-light, the whole craft weighing about 7 ounces (200 g)! Starwisp carries no fuel, instead it is blown through the Solar System by a space-powered station sending out a beam of microwaves. These are no more than a form of radiation, but they could focus enough pressure on the Starwisp to boost it to a high speed quickly. Calculations show the probe would move along at more than 40,000 miles a second (60,000 km/sec) in a few days, after which the power station would be switched off. Even at this speed, it's still a 21-year mission to Alpha Centauri, the closest star system.

## Triple-star target

Alpha Centauri is a group of three stars. One of them is much like our own Sun, while the smallest is a dim "red dwarf." We don't know if there are planets in the system, but when Starwisp is built, a space telescope will be able to see any planets that exist, so Starwisp will have a target to explore.

*Starwisp is light but large. Here the probe is compared in size with two of the world's tallest buildings, Kuala Lumpur's Petronas Towers and the Eiffel Tower in Paris.*

*Starwisp flies through the Alpha Centauri system in only a few hours, beaming pictures back to Earth. If the idea works, we could send more robot explorers to other star systems.*

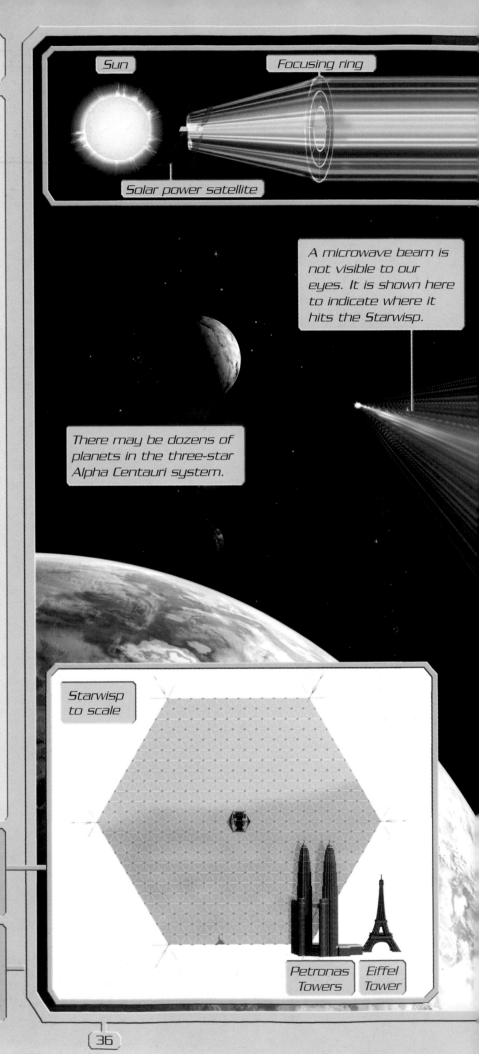

Sun

Focusing ring

Solar power satellite

A microwave beam is not visible to our eyes. It is shown here to indicate where it hits the Starwisp.

There may be dozens of planets in the three-star Alpha Centauri system.

Starwisp to scale

Petronas Towers

Eiffel Tower

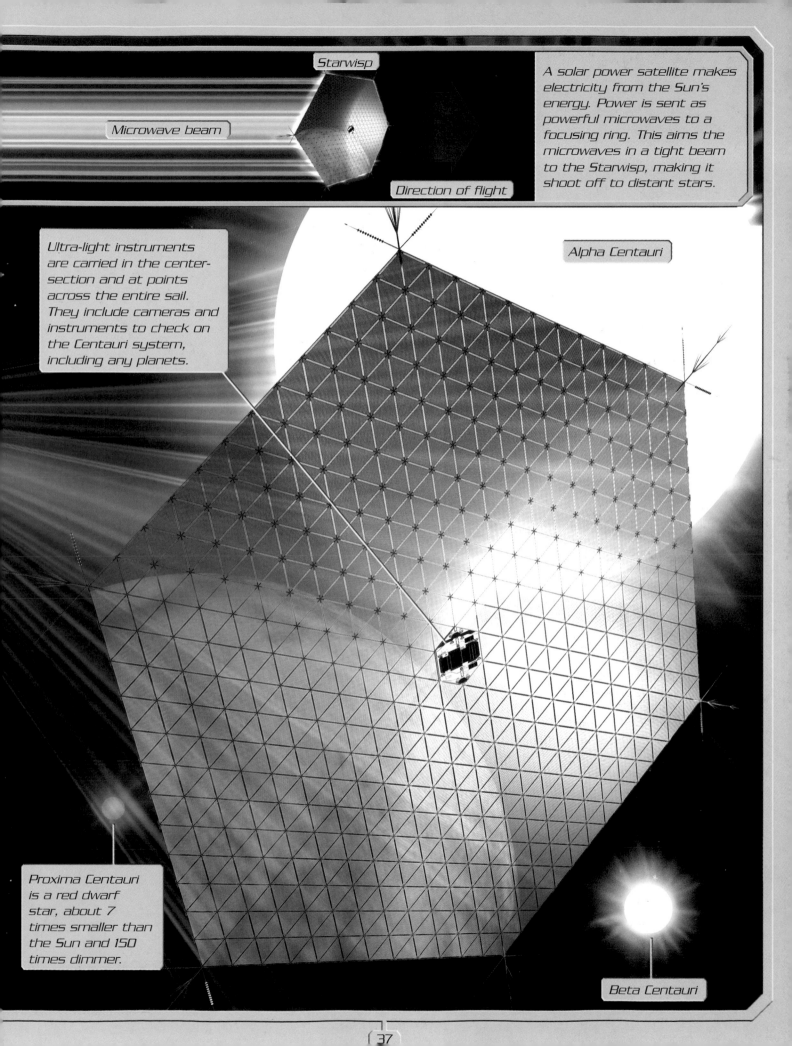

Starwisp

Microwave beam

Direction of flight

A solar power satellite makes electricity from the Sun's energy. Power is sent as powerful microwaves to a focusing ring. This aims the microwaves in a tight beam to the Starwisp, making it shoot off to distant stars.

Ultra-light instruments are carried in the center-section and at points across the entire sail. They include cameras and instruments to check on the Centauri system, including any planets.

Alpha Centauri

Proxima Centauri is a red dwarf star, about 7 times smaller than the Sun and 150 times dimmer.

Beta Centauri

# DEATH OF A WORLD

If starprobes are ever built, there won't be any shortage of places to send them. Our local "star city," the Milky Way galaxy, contains more than 100 billion stars. Many of these stars have planets, so researchers will have plenty of interesting sights to see in our local galactic neighborhood.

## Searching for life

At present, we don't know of other planets where there is life, besides Earth. But with so many stars and planets out there – by 2002 more than 100 planets had been found circling other stars – it seems unlikely that life on Earth is unique. Most researchers think there will be some form of life out there, even if there are no intelligent aliens like those in sci-fi movies. If space telescopes find Earth-like planets with breathable air and oceans, these will be targets for star probes.

## Late arrival

Just because a planet has life does not mean things stay that way. Huge cosmic events occur from time to time, killing whole species. Space rocks have hit our planet many times – about 65 million years ago, such a collision will have caused the dinosaurs' extinction. Sending a starprobe is one way to find alien life.

## Planetary funeral

On the right, a future starprobe is shown exploring a dying world. The twin stars (far top right) are throwing out vast amounts of heat and light that are slowly reducing the planet's surface to a bubbling sea of molten rock. If anything is still alive down there, the starprobe has only a short time to find it.

*Some stars explode with a force far greater than the biggest nuclear weapon. A pattern of glowing gas is all that remains of supernova 1987a.*

*The two stars of this distant star system spin closely together. Trails of glowing gases expand into space. Here, a future starprobe explores a nearby planet before it is destroyed completely by the heat.*

*Instruments on the starprobe show a huge spiral of gases spinning out from the two stars. To our eyes, the view would be less spectacular – the spiral would have only a faint misty appearance.*

*Starprobe flies by at high speed to avoid overheating.*

These stars spin so closely that they have pulled each other into distorted egg shapes.

On planet Earth there are bacteria that live in hot rocks and boiling geysers, so there might be alien creatures that can survive on this ultra-hot world.

Thick shielding protects instruments in the probe.

Other worlds may face an endless winter when their sun eventually runs out of fuel and grows cold. Then the challenge for alien life would be how to survive on a planet in deep-freeze.

# A NEW EARTH?

Could we live on Venus? It Is su hot and poisonous there that the idea of survival sounds impossible. Yet in the distant future, we might be able to change the air and climate to make Venus much more comfortable.

## Tough bugs

One idea is to build a fleet of robot probes to "seed" the atmosphere of Venus with billions of special bacteria, created in the laboratory for one job, to change the atmosphere. The bacteria, actually a type of algae, would feed off carbon dioxide gas in the atmosphere of Venus, releasing their waste as oxygen, a gas vital to humans. The air-change would not be a quick job – it could take centuries – but at last the air would clear a little and Venus could start to cool off as heat escapes.

## More water

Eventually the first rain could fall, and soon the surface of Venus would have ponds and lakes. However, scientists believe that the air of Venus holds only enough water vapor to create a knee-deep ocean. A plan to provide more water calls for robo-craft to divert the paths of some comets containing large amounts of water-ice. If such a comet were sent on a course that grazes the upper air of Venus, it would melt in moments, sending a huge spray of water vapor into the atmosphere. One day, robots and humans might succeed in turning Venus into a second Earth.

*Probe releases oxygen-making bacteria into the upper air.*

*Some scientists think that life may already exist in the clouds about 30 miles (50 km) high. If we found microbes, then we would need to study them first, before trying to change their environment.*

**Spacecraft of the bacteria fleet leave Earth orbit, on course for Venus. The journey there will take only a few months, but the project itself may last for many years.**

**Small seed-probes fly into the atmosphere of Venus. They release clouds of tough bacteria as they go.**

**A lightweight but tough Venus-rover checks on how conditions are starting to change on the surface. Here rain falls onto the cooling rocks for the very first time.**

When empty, the seed-probe flies back to its transporter ship for return to Earth. After being refilled with bacteria, the probe will be ready for another seeding flight.

In the upper atmosphere of Venus, temperatures are much cooler than at ground level.

Automatic flip-out panels

Seed tubes filled with bacteria

Engine for returning to the transporter craft, which waits in Venus orbit

# REBEL ROBOT

Intelligent robots sound like science fiction, and robots attacking humans sounds even more ridiculous. Computers perform calculations faster each year, and become more powerful. Eventually robotic machines might develop a form of "intelligence," and this could equal or exceed that of human beings. Some scientists believe this is a danger to humanity – after all, intelligent robots might not want to take orders from "inferior" humans. Or they may simply calculate that humans are too dirty and unintelligent to have around.

## Battle in space

Command of near-Earth space is already a top priority for present-day military planners. Since the 1960s, satellites have been used to check on such things as nuclear-bomb tests, and the positions of enemy forces. In the near future, laser-equipped satellites might be able to shoot down enemy missiles. Beyond this, intelligent robots could be sent on military missions right on the front lines.

## Invisible attacker

One space hazard is deadly radiation from the Sun. Humans need a lot of protection, like the Earth's ozone layer. Computers and electronic systems are also vulnerable if left unshielded. In the future, a sudden burst of intense radiation could scramble the control circuits of a military space robot, and cause it to start shooting at the wrong target. If several robots are involved, there might be an army of killer machines on the loose, rampaging completely out of control. Of course, at this point, it's all science fiction.

*Military satellites have been used for many years, especially for checking enemy troop movements.*

*Deadly weapons may be placed in Earth orbit as soon as 2010. Firing commands will be controlled largely done by computers.*

*Warrior robots go hunting in this sci-fi vision of the future. Their prey – humans on a colony planet.*

*Sealed domes allow humans to live on this alien world, while the air is being slowly changed to a breathable mixture. Once a dome is breached, the humans inside are in deadly peril.*

*Clawed metal feet for good grip on rough surfaces*

The tough metal and plastic body is very heavily armored for protection, making the robot almost invincible.

Warrior robot is armed with powerful laser weapons.

# SPACE-TIME ZONE

In the half-century since the launch of Sputnik 1 in 1957, robot explorers have been launched into space by the hundreds. Early spacecraft designers worked very hard to achieve success in robotics.

## Design targets

Space pioneers had three main goals. The first was to get a probe into space, because early rockets often blew up or went astray before reaching space. The second goal was to be accurate. Electronic systems that could guide a probe with pinpoint-accuracy to a distant, moving space target took many years to develop. The third design goal, reliability, was just as important as the first two. It doesn't help to get a probe to a distant planet if it breaks down along the way. Most of our home electronic machines (TV, hi-fi, computers, and so on) owe their reliability to early space efforts.

## Robot travelers

Despite all the improvements, things still go wrong from time to time. A satellite might go into the wrong orbit, or a Mars probe might disappear for no apparent reason. But despite this, robot explorers have successfully traveled across much of the Solar System. And in the future, they may send information about far stars, exo-planets, and strange environments.

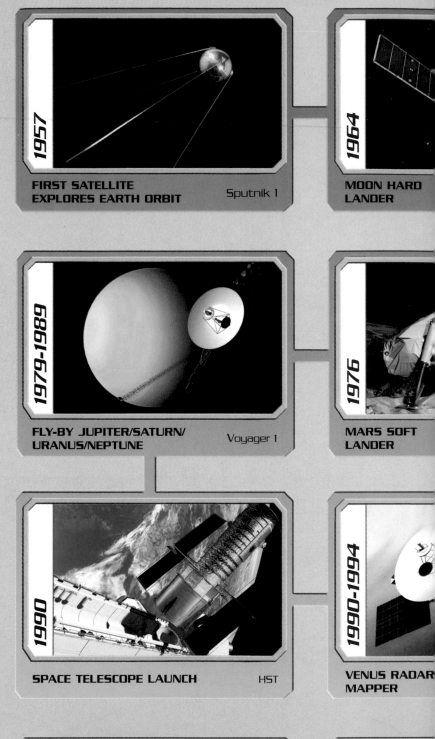

**1957**

**FIRST SATELLITE EXPLORES EARTH ORBIT**     Sputnik 1

**1964**

**MOON HARD LANDER**

**1979–1989**

**FLY-BY JUPITER/SATURN/ URANUS/NEPTUNE**     Voyager 1

**1976**

**MARS SOFT LANDER**

**1990**

**SPACE TELESCOPE LAUNCH**     HST

**1990–1994**

**VENUS RADAR MAPPER**

**c. 2020?**

**UNDER THE ICE OF EUROPA**     Space sub

**c. 2015?**

**PLUTO FLY-BY**     New Horizons

**2011**

**COMET LANDIN**

Ranger 7

**1970**
**VENUS SOFT LANDER** Venera 7

**1970**
**RUSSIAN MOON ROVER** Lunokhod

Viking 1, 2

**1974**
**MERCURY FLY-BY** Mariner 10

**1973**
**JUPITER FLY-BY** Pioneer 10

Magellan

**1997**
**MARS ROVER** Sojourner

**2004**
**ARRIVAL SATURN SYSTEM** Cassini

Rosetta

**2008-2013**
**SEARCH FOR EARTH-SIZED EXO-PLANETS** James Webb Space Telescope

**2007-2010**
**MERCURY FLY-BY AND ORBIT** Messenger

# GLOSSARY

**asteroid** One of many rocky objects that did not become a planet when the Solar System was formed. There are thousands of asteroids, many of them in a belt between the planets Mars and Jupiter. The biggest asteroids are round, like mini-worlds. The smallest are all sorts of shapes, from ovals to peanuts.

**atmosphere** The gases that surround a planet. The Earth's is made up mainly of the gases nitrogen and oxygen. Other planets have completely different gas mixtures, which we cannot breathe. In space, there is no air at all, so a crewed spacecraft has to take its own air supply.

**bacteria** Very simple forms of life that consist of just a single cell (unlike humans, who are made of billions of cells, like bricks in a wall). Some types of simple plant life called algae are single-celled.

**carbon dioxide** A gas found in the atmosphere of many planets. It is the gas that humans breathe out.

**Cassini** A spaceprobe aimed at the planet Saturn and its moons, especially Titan. The probe is named after the Italian astronomer Gian Domenico Cassini, who studied the planet and its rings in the 1600s.

**Centauri system** The nearest star group to our own local star, the Sun. The Centauri system consists of three stars – Alpha, Beta, and Proxima. Scientists have so far found one planet there, and likely more exist.

**comet** A space body, made of a frozen mixture of ice, rock, and dust, that has a very long orbit around the Sun. When a comet gets near the Sun, the heat may vaporize some of its matter to form long tails of gas and dust. Some comets break up when this has happened enough times.

**crater** A circular hole in the surface of a planet, moon, or asteroid, made by the impact of a meteor crashing into the ground. May also be made by a volcano.

**cryobot** A type of probe that uses heat to melt through ice.

**European Space Agency (ESA)** Large research organization, backed by many countries in Europe. It is a European version of NASA.

**exo-planet** A planet of a solar system outside our own: short for "extra-solar planet."

**flare** A sudden burst of energy on the Sun. A prominence is a type of flare.

**fly-by** Name for a space mission that is designed to go close to a planet or moon, rather than go into orbit or land on the surface. Some fly-bys are also used to give the probe a boost in speed from the planet's gravitational pull.

**fossil, fossilized** The hardened remains of a plant or animal that has been preserved from the past, usually millions of years.

**galaxy** A vast collection of stars, turning in space. Our Solar System is a part of the Milky Way galaxy, which is spiral-shaped and contains about 100 billion stars. Other galaxies come in various shapes and sizes. Latest calculations suggest that there are more than 50 billion galaxies in the visible universe.

**gas-giant** A large planet that consists mostly of gases, rather than having a rocky surface with a separate atmosphere like Earth. Jupiter, Saturn, Uranus, and Neptune are all gas-giants.

**Grand Tour** The four-planet fly-by carried out by the Voyager 2 spaceprobe, which took pictures of Jupiter, Saturn, Uranus, and Neptune. The term Grand Tour was first used for the custom of visiting the countries of Europe, one after the other.

**gravity** The unseen force that keeps us firmly on the Earth. In orbit, gravity is much less, but it is not exactly "zero." The correct term for orbiting craft and crew is that they are in "free-fall" or "microgravity." Gravity varies according to how much matter, or "mass" an object contains. On the Moon (a lighter object than the Earth) gravity is six times less. On Jupiter (a heavier object), it is much more.

**Great Red Spot (GRS)** A stormy area on Jupiter big enough to blanket the Earth three times. It has been seen by astronomers for over 300 years. Voyager 2 found that the planet Neptune also has a storm-spot, named the Great Dark Spot (GDR).

**Huygens** Lander-probe carried by the Cassini orbiter-probe, built to parachute down to the surface of Saturn's moon Titan. The lander is named after the Dutch scientist Christiaan Huygens, who in 1655 discovered that Saturn was surrounded by huge rings. Today we know that they are made of countless ice particles, ranging in size from boulders to grains of dust. All the gas-giant planets have rings, but Saturn's are the most spectacular.

**Kuiper Belt Object (KBO)** One of the billions of rock-and-ice chunks that exist far beyond the orbit of Pluto. Researchers think that most comets come from this space-zone.

**light-year (ly)** The distance that light travels in one year, at a speed of 186,000 miles per second (300,000 km/sec). The Solar System's nearest star neighbor is the Alpha Centauri triple-star system, which is a little more than four light years away.

**lunar** To do with the Moon, after its Latin name, Luna.

**meteor** Dust and rock particles that fly through space at 45 miles per second (72 km/sec) or more. Small ones burn up as they hit the Earth's atmosphere, when they can often be seen on a clear night as a brief streak of light crossing the sky. Bigger ones may form a circular crater if they hit the Earth or other space object.

**microwave** A type of radiation that can be used to heat food. It has also been suggested as a way of beaming energy across space to a starprobe.

**module** General name for a major section of a spacecraft. An example is the payload module carried by a launch rocket.

**Moon** Earth's natural satellite, which orbits some 238,000 miles (384,000 km) away. The other planets (except Mercury and Venus) also have moons. These vary in size and number. Mars has just two tiny ones, but Jupiter has at least 52 moons.

**nucleus** The core of a comet, thought to be mostly rock, with gas, dust, and ice mixed in.

**orbit** The curving path (circular or oval) in space that an object takes around another. It applies to the orbit of our Earth around the Sun, as well as to a spacecraft around the Earth, or a spaceprobe around another planet or moon.

**radar** An electronic system that sends out a radio beam. Part of the beam may bounce off a solid object in its path, showing the reflection as a "return" on a TV screen. Radar beams can pass easily through mist and cloud, so were used to map the surface of the cloudy planet Venus by the U.S. Magellan probe.

**radiation** A term for the "electromagnetic spectrum" in which you find light, radio waves, cosmic rays, x-rays, infra-red, and more. If living tissue receives too much radiation, cell damage, and cancer may be caused.

**red dwarf** A type of small star that glows only a dim red, giving out only a little heat and light. Many of the Sun's neighbors are red dwarfs, including the nearest star of all, Proxima Centauri, the smallest of the three stars in the Centauri system.

**rover** General word for any spaceprobe that is built to move around on another space object. As an example, the Marsprobe Sojourner carried a small wheeled rover called "Rocky."

**satellite** Any object that orbits around another world in space. An "artificial" satellite is an orbiter made by humans, as opposed to a "natural" satellite, such as the Moon, which circles the Earth.

**sensor** A spacecraft instrument that views or measures, such as a camera or a thermometer.

**solar** To do with the Sun, after its Latin name, Sol.

**solar panel** Flat electronic panels that convert the energy in light to electricity. They are used a great deal in spacecraft as they provide free electrical power by using light from the Sun. They are sometimes called a photovoltaic array.

**Solar System** The group of nine planets and their moons that orbit around the Sun. There are also many smaller objects, such as asteroids and comets. Many other stars with planets have been discovered, though researchers have not yet found a planet similar to Earth.

**spaceprobe** An uncrewed spacecraft sent to study planets, moons, comets, and other objects in the universe.

**Space Shuttle** U.S.-built craft that carries humans into space, though only as far as orbit around the Earth. Also used as a space "truck" to haul satellites and other loads.

**space telescope** A telescope used to look at objects in deep space. The best known is the Hubble Space Telescope (HST), which has been in orbit around the Earth since 1990. It was named after a famous U.S. astronomer, Edwin Hubble, and will be used until about 2010.

**star** A hot, glowing ball of gas in space. The Sun is our local star, the temperature at its visible surface being 10,430°F (5777°C).

**Sputnik** Word used to describe some early Russian spaceprobes. It means "little star." Sputnik 1 was the first craft to be launched into Earth orbit, in 1957.

**vacuum** Literally, no air. Most of space is a vacuum, although radiation of various forms is always present.

# INDEX